GOLD RUSH!
EL DORADO IN BRITISH COLUMBIA

KATHRYN BRIDGE

**CANADIAN MUSEUM OF HISTORY
MUSÉE CANADIEN DE L'HISTOIRE**

Library and Archives Canada
Cataloguing in Publication

Bridge, Kathryn Anne, author
Gold rush! : El Dorado in British Columbia /
Kathryn Bridge.

(Souvenir catalogue series, ISSN 2291-6385; 14)
Issued also in French under title: Ruée vers l'or!
ISBN 978-0-660-03142-2 (paperback)
Cat. no.: NM23-5/14-2016E

1. Gold mines and mining – British Columbia
    – History.
2. British Columbia – Gold discoveries.
3. British Columbia – History – 1849-1871.
I. Canadian Museum of History, issuing body.
II. Title.
III. Series: Souvenir catalogue series; 14.

FC3820.G6B75 2016
971.1'02
C2016-900917-3

Published by the
Canadian Museum of History
100 Laurier Street
Gatineau, QC K1A 0M8
historymuseum.ca

Printed and bound in Canada.

This work is a souvenir of the exhibition
Gold Rush! – El Dorado in British Columbia,
which was organized by the Royal BC Museum,
in collaboration with the Canadian Museum
of History.

Cover image:
AVprophoto, S_Photo & Triff / Shutterstock.com

Souvenir Catalogue series, 14
ISSN 2291-6385

Contents

FOREWORD

The mystique of gold has persisted for 6,000 years. Once a sacred symbol viewed by Indigenous peoples of South America as representing the transformative power within all beings, gold has come to signify wealth and power.

Contemporary societies prize gold medals, gold records and gold wedding rings, and the word itself has become imbued with the suggestion of wealth, achievement and prestige.

Yet gold has historically had a much greater impact than its symbolic or mythological significance would suggest. Throughout history and across the globe, gold has been a powerfully transformative force, with a major material impact on landscapes and communities.

Miner using a rocker box, Barkerville, 1868

So it was with the great gold rushes of the 19th century. These involved massive migrations of fortune-seekers, causing both physical transformation and social upheaval to new frontiers in California, Australia, British Columbia and the Klondike. These waves of human displacement breathed life into upstart cities such as Victoria, Melbourne and San Francisco. They also brought violence and conflict — often played out in "instant" miner settlements, where disputes were commonly settled with vigilante justice.

Gold Rush! – El Dorado in British Columbia offers an engaging and detailed account of how these processes unfolded in Canada's far west, beginning in 1858 along the Fraser River, and later in the Cariboo region and beyond. Organized by the Royal British Columbia Museum in collaboration with the Canadian Museum of History, **Gold Rush!** is an up-close encounter with the people and events animating the frenetic years when fortunes were won and lost, and the dreams of desperate people were routinely dashed.

The journey through the BC gold rush presents crucial keys to an understanding of today's British Columbia. The province's modern multiculturalism has roots in that earlier influx of prospectors and merchants from all over the world, many of whom stayed behind after gold fever subsided.

Current relations between First Nations and non-Aboriginal British Columbia were also shaped by gold rush clashes that largely overturned the spirit of conciliation that had characterized the fur-trade era. The environmental impact of resource extraction was also a concern, both then and now.

El Dorado is an ancient myth. Its influence, however, persists to this day.

Jean-Marc Blais
Director General
Canadian Museum
of History

Jack Lohman
Chief Executive Officer
Royal British Columbia
Museum

Wheel and flumes at the Davis claim on William's Creek, 1867

INTRODUCTION

In 1858 a great wave of humanity poured into the area we now call British Columbia. By all accounts 30,000 gold seekers — mostly men — arrived within the first few months and many others followed over the next five years.

News of gold — of a "New El Dorado" — spurred a rush that changed forever the ways of life for First Nations inhabitants and those already settled in or around fur-trading posts. Most of the early gold seekers arrived at Fort Victoria, Vancouver Island, via ocean-going vessels from San Francisco.

From there they journeyed across the Strait of Georgia to the mainland and on to Fort Yale, at the head of navigation on the Fraser River. Thousands more came overland from California, through Oregon and Washington territories, and followed native trails and river courses northward to the gold fields.

The gold rush has received much attention from historians and local history buffs. Books, websites, museums and historical highway signs tell stories about the rush and the movements of gold seekers north along the Fraser River into the Cariboo. Barkerville, now a national heritage site in the Cariboo, along with a series of small settlements — the original historical stopping houses for changing horses along the Cariboo Wagon Road — and towns such as Lytton, Lillooet, Spences Bridge and Boston Bar are reminders of this transitional chapter in British Columbia's history.

Place names associated with the gold rush are fast disappearing with depopulation, however. In years past, the Province of British Columbia supported and established historical stops of interest that preserved homes and ranches of the immediate post-rush period as heritage properties. Places like Hat Creek Ranch (near Cache Creek), Ashcroft Manor and Cottonwood House survive in their architecture and settings as physical reminders of the scale of settler achievements.

Tourism BC promotes the Gold Rush Trail, and the New Pathways to Gold Society supports economic growth through heritage tourism, First Nations reconciliation, community projects and events.

The "instant" society created by a gold rush held very distinct characteristics and its own complexities. Most visibly, the population was about 90% male. White women — the wives, daughters, business owners and, yes, miners — lived in a dominantly male society. It was also a very young colonial society, the average age well below 30.

And it was multicultural — people from around the globe shared a dream to strike it rich. English was not the only language spoken; French, Spanish, Chinese and German were likely to be heard on the trails, on the gravel bars of the river and in the settlements.

Races, classes and cultures mixed in unprecedented ways. For First Nations people living in the area, the gold rush was an intimate experience. Some participated as miners, all endured racism and many suffered violent acts committed by gold seekers, and often retaliated.

Understanding the gold rush requires learning from the multiple perspectives of those who experienced it. Today's British Columbia is formed in part from multicultural roots and as a legacy of the gold seekers who stayed on.

Kathryn Bridge
Curator, History and Art
Royal British Columbia Museum

Dr. Kathryn Bridge is a historian, archivist and curator at the Royal British Columbia Museum. She has written several books on historical figures in BC, including *By Snowshoe, Buckboard and Steamer* (about BC's frontier women), which won the 1998 Lieutenant-Governor's Medal for Historical Writing, and *Emily Carr in England* (2014). Dr. Bridge is also the editor of *New Perspectives on the Gold Rush*, published by the Royal BC Museum in 2015.

Nugget, crystalline gold

OUR HISTORY, WROUGHT IN GOLD

What happens to a world driven by a myth?

Gold and gold seekers changed the world. Gold rushes drove exploration, conquest and colonization. El Dorado, the legendary source of limitless gold, wove a bright thread through the Western world's imagination for centuries.

The myth of El Dorado drove massive migrations to gold rushes around the planet. But British Columbia's rush was different. First Nations played a key role, as did immigrants from China and other countries. Desire — for gold, for a better life — created a colony and then shaped it into a province.

Gold's impact continues today, sparking new stories, shaping the land. Gold affects your life, just as it did so many others.

400 ounce gold bars

El Dorado: The myth of gold

How far would you travel for what you desire?

Spanish explorers voyaged to South America in the 15th and 16th centuries looking for riches. They found what looked like vast collections of gold. Indigenous societies had mined and amassed the metal, creating intricate ritual objects, figurines and jewellery.

Spanish conquistadors looted the treasures, returning to Europe with stolen gold and stories of endless wealth. The golden objects were melted down. But for Europeans, the stories lived on. El Dorado held the promise of endless gold, hiding somewhere in the New World. But did the Americas actually contain these mountains or cities of gold?

The myth goes global

No one found the land of endless gold, yet the myth continued to grow. European treasure seekers pillaged South America and Mexico. Conquest displaced cultures and devastated populations through disease and warfare.

Three hundred years after the conquistadors, miners discovered placer gold in California. This is gold in its raw form: flakes and nuggets found in the placer — the gravel — of stream beds. Thousands of people flocked to California, then to Australia and British Columbia. The myth of endless gold fuelled each 19th century rush.

The search continues today.

Haida box by Bill Reid, 1971

Bill Reid (1920–1998) was the great nephew
of Haida artist da.a.xiigang, Charles Edenshaw
(1839–1920), and the grandson of carver
Charles Gladstone (1878–1954), who was
trained by Edenshaw. Reid grew up in Victoria,
worked as a CBC announcer in Toronto and
trained as a jeweller. He produced a number of
modernist pieces in gold, turning to Haida-style
carving and graphic design in the late 1950s
after being inspired by a visit to Haida Gwaii.
For this small gold box, made in 1971, he used
jewellers' techniques to render Haida forms
drawn from traditional carving and form-line
designs influenced by Haida tradition.

THE ALLURE OF GOLD

Was El Dorado a golden city, a mountain of gold or a gold-covered man returning metal to the earth? Was it story or fact, appearance or reality?

When Europeans found gold in South America, it appeared endless. But they didn't realize how long it had taken the native inhabitants to find, collect and shape the raw metal into objects of beauty. In reality, El Dorado was millions of gold fragments painstakingly amassed over centuries. Spanish explorers only saw the final abundance.

The gold was real; the myth, elusive. The lure of golden wealth inspired people to explore, to conquer, to rush all over the world.

Miners in the Sierra

Norton Bush, oil on canvas, 1869

Bright, beautiful and transformative

South America's golden jewellery and icons had spiritual and symbolic meanings, rather than monetary value. Indigenous peoples used gold when burying the dead. Gold symbolized the transformative power in all beings. To the Inca, this rare and precious metal represented the power of their gods and the sun.

Beyond its beauty, gold offers durability. It doesn't easily corrode, yet it's soft and pliable for a metal — perfect for jewellers and artists. Part of the gold you wear today may have been stolen from a Colombian chief or an Egyptian king, or mined in Mexico's Sierra Madre. Melted and reused again and again, gold circles the world.

Trading and travelling the world

The earliest known golden artifacts are 6,000 years old, from a gravesite near Varna, Bulgaria. The first gold coins were minted almost 3,000 years ago in Anatolia (where Turkey is today).

Kingdoms and empires rose and fell based on the control of gold, which merchants used as an international system of trade. Trade routes carried gold and golden objects all over the world. For thousands of years our fascination with gold has shaped where we go, what we exchange and how we explore.

The fever spreads

The legend of El Dorado fired much of the world's imagination, shaping explorers' journeys and, eventually, immigrant travel during gold rushes. In turn, the desire for gold forever changed Indigenous societies throughout Colombia and the rest of the Americas. Traditional ways of life disappeared. As gold became a currency, its spiritual link faded.

Explorers and gold seekers brought racism, violence and disease, spreading them among Indigenous peoples. From Colombia to Australia, California to British Columbia, life would never be the same.

The Lone Prospector

Albertus D. O. Browere,
oil on canvas, 30 x 50 in., 1853

Golden eagle carving from the side paddle box of the SS *Brother Jonathan*

The ship made regular runs between Victoria and San Francisco during the British Columbia gold rush.

THE HISTORY OF GOLD RUSHES

Gold fever went global in the 19th century, with gold rushes causing the first voluntary large-scale world migrations.

Masses of people from Europe, Asia and the Americas joined each rush, travelling to Australia, New Zealand, California and British Columbia. All races, ages and classes felt the pull to better their lives.

In the 1800s, transportation by ship was easier than ever before. News of the next El Dorado spread like wildfire. Ports like Hong Kong grew as Chinese joined the rushes and their search for El Dorado. The arrival of so many people overwhelmed the far corners of the world.

Why study a gold rush?

The gold rush made Canada a Pacific Rim nation — the rush connected the West to the rest of the world. It also sparked immigration. The West's first Chinese and Black settlers arrived; the oldest Jewish community formed. Quebec miners met French gold seekers on the Fraser River. People gathered from Australia, Chile, Hungary, Italy, Mexico and elsewhere.

The rush was a source of the West's deepest wounds: violence, racism and injustice. It is a story of lost and gained homelands, war and peace treaties, mingling cultures and a new commonwealth.

Some say that Western Canada began with the railway. In fact, it began with a gold rush.

Going for the gold

Fortune-seeking became a rite of passage for young men, and some women. They sprinted from rush to rush, El Dorado driving them on. The first to arrive had the pick of the gold fields. Latecomers got the dregs or nothing at all. The game of chance was open to everyone.

California saw the century's first great rush in 1849. Then, in 1852, people raced to Australia. British Columbia's first major rush, along the Fraser River, began in 1858. Miners followed gold to the Cariboo region and beyond. The last 19th century rush, the Klondike Stampede, occurred in 1897 in what is now the Yukon.

Slim Jim or ***The Parson Takes the Pot***
Rowland Lee, oil on canvas, 1892

Note the bag of gold coins on the gambler's lap
and gold coins used in this poker game. Saloons,
high stakes card games and professional gamblers
followed in the wave of the gold rush.

THE NEW EL DORADO;
or,
BRITISH COLUMBIA.

BY
KINAHAN CORNWALLIS,
AUTHOR OF "PANAMA LISBON," "HOWARD PLANTAGENET," &c. &c.

WITH A MAP AND ILLUSTRATION BY THE AUTHOR.

LONDON:
THOMAS CAUTLEY NEWBY, PUBLISHER,
30. WELBECK STREET.
1858.

Golden California

A mill worker discovered California gold on the American River in 1848. Within a year the world arrived! More than 800 ships full of miners docked in 1849, transforming San Francisco from a sleepy village into a boom town.

Not everyone received a warm welcome. Chinese and Latin American miners faced discrimination and intolerance and had to pay a steep Foreign Miners Tax.

Newly arrived American gold seekers displaced Spanish and Mexican settlers, and drove Latin Americans and Chinese from their claims. Native Americans lost their land and their rights, as they were forced onto reservations. Some were massacred by miner-militias. Crime and vigilante justice soared as gold grew harder to find.

The New El Dorado, or British Columbia

Kinahan Cornwallis wrote an idyllic description of the Fraser River goldfields in 1858, luring many naïve adventurers.

Australian fever

Australia's 1852 gold-rush violence echoed California's. British soldiers killed over 20 miners during the Eureka rebellion in Ballarat in 1854. They rebelled after the acquittal of a hotel keeper who had been accused of murdering a miner. Australia was a British colony with expensive, mandatory mining licenses and no guaranteed right to vote or own land. Was the acquittal just another example of unjust British rule?

Thousands of angry miners built a stockade, burned licenses and hoisted an independent flag. Soon after, the government sent in soldiers.

Aboriginal populations in Australia also suffered. Racism and violence spread as immigrants flooded in. New diseases and alcohol claimed many lives. Gold enriched Australia, but the cost was high.

Blow pan

For separating fine gold from sand.

An Australian gold diggings

Edwin Roper Stocqueler, oil on canvas,
70.5 x 90.3 cm, c. 1855 (detail)

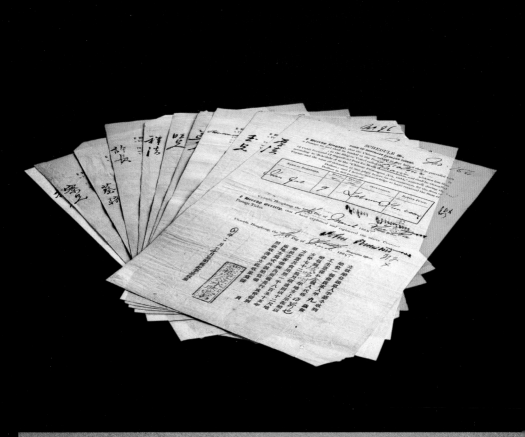

Gold Mountain dream

As the search for gold grew global, other myths drew gold seekers. Gold Mountain (金山, *gum saan*) is a Chinese term for a land of promise, opportunity and wealth. Originally, Gold Mountain was the destination in a cautionary folk tale. Those who tried to find it were punished for their greed. When myth became reality, San Francisco became Gold Mountain City (金山大埠) in the 1850s.

As the Australia rush began, Melbourne became New Gold Mountain. Then it was British Columbia's Fraser River. Every young man dreamed of becoming a Gold Mountain Sojourner (金山客, *gum saan haak*), cherished as a husband, son-in-law or business partner.

Tickets for passage on the *Maria* from Hong Kong to Victoria, 1865

Conditions were appalling for the 316 Chinese men and boys — one meal per day and a sleeping space of only 14 inches (35 cm), illegal under the *Chinese Passengers Act* of 1855.

"In-between places" in the Pacific

Gold rushes of the 19th century shaped and reshaped trans-Pacific networks of migration and commerce. In the process, Hong Kong, Canton, San Francisco, Victoria (and later Vancouver), Sydney and other Pacific ports developed into what historian Elizabeth Sinn (University of Hong Kong) calls "in-between places." These places played a key role in maintaining the vibrant flow of people, goods, funds, "commercial intelligence," correspondence and even dead bodies and bones.

They sometimes became second homes to Chinese migrants. Chinese merchants, shopkeepers, artisans, cooks and doctors — not just "coolie" labourers — all played active roles in different aspects of the social, economic and cultural exchanges across the Pacific.

Hand-forged mining tools

Comparative gold rushes

The 19th century gold rushes increased the world's gold supply and stimulated global trade and investment. For most individuals, whatever their origins, gold mining was not a profitable adventure.

Nevertheless, gold seekers from many parts of Europe, the Americas and Asia followed the gold trail around the Pacific Rim from California to Australia, New Zealand and British Columbia. Dr. Keir Reeves (Federation University Australia) has pointed out that Chinese migration was similar to that of European and other gold seekers. Some left, and others helped create new settler communities.

Did gold mean life?

Gold seekers also left their homelands because of political turmoil, violence or discrimination. Failed harvests, overpopulation and the need to support family pushed many to travel.

People emigrated to find not only wealth and adventure but also better living conditions and social freedoms. More ocean-going ships meant greater access for all. Family networks or wealthy merchants advanced money for a miner's passage. Many found gold, and some set up businesses. Others did anything they could to pay their debt and survive.

Gold pan, Barkerville

Blackened with soot to make gold more visible.

A watery world

You can't mine for gold without water. Miners panned for surface gold in rivers and streams, using water to rinse away the worthless gravel. Others dug for gold in the ground, looking for buried ancient streams. Water helped carve the soil and wash it away.

Prospecting for Alluvial Gold in British Columbia

William G. R. Hind, oil on canvas, 1864

If water was your ally, it could also be your enemy. Mine shafts flooded. Rivers rose and covered gold-bearing gravel bars. Could water reveal the source of the nuggets and veins, the mother lode?

Gold mining technology

Systems of gold-mining technology spread quickly from California to other gold rushes. The first arrivals used simple tools, such as a smoke-blackened pan to wash river gravel and expose gold nuggets. Groups of partners built rocker boxes and sluices. Shareholders bought claims and water rights, hired labourers and invested in complex sluices, flumes, mine shafts and tunnels. Large companies invested in creek diversions or hydraulic mining that destroyed river banks, valleys or hillsides.

Each level of technology moves more gravel per day. Each has a higher cost of entry. Low-cost tools invite easy entry and mobility. The harder it is to find gold, the more earth you need to move — costs rise along with the environmental destruction.

Handmade miner's tunnel cart,
Barkerville, 1860s

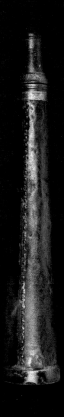

Hydraulic nozzle,
Barkerville

How would you fare in the gold rush?

How would you fare if you couldn't understand your neighbours' language? What if everything was unfamiliar: landscape, people, rules, even the food you ate? Would you feel lonely, frightened or free?

With few women and children in the gold fields, men took on chores like cooking and washing. People had to work together in new ways. A gold rush shook up the social order. Class, race and cultural differences often mattered less than survival. Conflict and partnership, greed and opportunity all surfaced during this harsh period of social transformation.

Miners, BC

William G. R. Hind, oil on canvas, 1860s

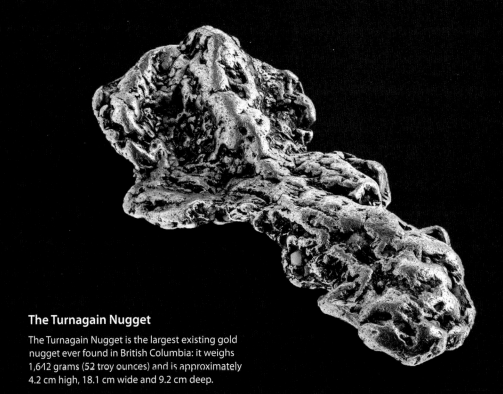

The Turnagain Nugget

The Turnagain Nugget is the largest existing gold nugget ever found in British Columbia: it weighs 1,612 grams (52 troy ounces) and is approximately 4.2 cm high, 18.1 cm wide and 9.2 cm deep.

Nuggets and veins

Imagine finding gold nuggets and flakes in the gravel at a river's edge. This is placer gold. Its discovery creates a rush, because the gold can be easily panned from the surface. But where does placer gold come from?

Lode deposits are veins of gold in rock that can only be extracted by mining. Rivers and streams erode lode deposits and carry the remnants downstream until they become caught in placer, the sand and gravel in the river bed. Beginning in 1858, prospectors along the Fraser River panned for placer gold. Moving north to the Cariboo, they mined for the mother lode — the source of the river's bounty.

All that glitters…

Many gold rushes featured darker aspects of human nature: greed, fraud, racism and violence. California miners waged war on Indigenous peoples, and vigilantes ruled. Miners in Australia shot Aboriginals and took up arms against the government, fighting a pitched battle with soldiers. British Columbia wasn't immune, but it aspired to be different. A gateway to the north, it had long-standing fur-trading partnerships with First Nations.

"Northern California has been the scene of a deliberate design to exterminate the Indian race… Some were infants at the breast, whose skulls had been cleft again and again. The whole number slaughtered in a single night was about two hundred and forty."

— "Indian Butcheries in California," *San Francisco Bulletin*, June 18, 1860

"The war has now fully commenced...
Every white man has full license
to shoot, kill, and destroy all
[aborigines...] The process... is so
slow, so painful, and so expensive...
that if the extermination of the
aboriginal races of Australia be
essential to the prosperity and
well-being of the European races,
then he is the greatest benefactor
to the country who mixes arsenic
in the ration flour and so destroys
them quietly and expeditiously."

— Editorial, *Maryborough Chronicle*,
  October 10, 1861

THE BRITISH COLUMBIA GOLD RUSH

The myths of El Dorado and Gold Mountain resurfaced with the discovery of Fraser River gold in 1858. The world's gaze turned to the place that would become British Columbia.

Over 30,000 people poured in from around the globe. Life in the territory changed forever, for First Nations and for the natural environment.

A fur-trade society, with deep partnerships between First Nations and Europeans, British Columbia was transformed under waves of immigrants and rampant adventurers. Both excitement and violence marked the era. The territory became the colony of British Columbia before the year was up. And just 13 years later, it joined Confederation as a province of Canada.

First Nations people near the Spences Bridge, Thompson River, 1864–1866

Healthy river, healthy salmon

Immigrants arriving during the gold rush didn't encounter an empty land. In British Columbia, First Nations civilizations were thousands of years old. Their lands held (and continue to hold) deep spiritual meanings, vibrant with history and culture.

Before the Fraser River rush, First Nations discovered, protected, mined and traded gold. But nothing was more important than the river's yearly salmon run — a major food source. Gold mining often disturbed rivers and threatened spawning grounds. When their resources — salmon, land, gold — were threatened, First Nations fought back.

An intimate partnership

Unlike those in California, Europeans and First Nations forged stable partnerships in the territory that would become British Columbia. Here, these civilizations met on intimate terms when fur traders married First Nations women. Men were glad to find wives. But the women also provided vital diplomatic relations, teaching their husbands local languages, travel routes and customs, and smoothing the way to peaceful co-existence.

Hudson's Bay Company coat of arms from the stern of the SS *Beaver*

The first steamship active along the northwest coast of North America, the SS *Beaver* carried fur traders and goods from 1836 to 1892.

The Hudson's Bay Company encouraged blended marriages with First Nations long before the gold rush. Partnerships strengthened at trading posts, where markets for salmon and furs, goods and arms could benefit all. When the gold rush began, these relationships would be critical.

First Nations mineral use

First Nations in British Columbia have used minerals for thousands of years. First Peoples knew where to find the different materials and understood their properties well. Minerals formed part of a traditional trade network that stretched across this region long before the fur trade. When First Nations learned of the trade interest in gold, they incorporated it into traditional trading systems and asserted their ownership and demands for control of access. Today, First Nations continue to participate with government in decision-making about resources.

Arrival of "the Hungry People"

British Columbia has been occupied
by Indigenous Peoples for millennia.
First Nations traded and shared the
resources of the land, the sea and
the great salmon rivers, in a complex
system of rights and prerogatives.
In 1858 thousands of gold seekers,
the *xwelitem* ("the Hungry People"),
arrived. The lives of First Nations
and their freedom to live on the
land and harvest its resources
changed forever.

Diary of James Nelles

James Nelles, from Grimsby, Ontario, walked from Port Douglas to the Cariboo in 1862. In June he wrote in his diary: "We are 11 days out from Lillooet and are 150 miles from that place... If the Miss Kitters [mosquitoes] (the only Misses we are troubled with) were not so cross would enjoy ourselves and tramp pretty well."

April 7th I washed m[...]
to day & find I am g[...]
my weight today [...]
3 lb heavier than [...]
before
8th Stmr Interfa[...]
up about 100 passen[...]
Been [...]
day — [...]
Catharine [...]
wed [...]
little [...]
expected [...]
y the Stmr but she [...]
the foreign mail. So [...]
for on next Stmr —
can guess where [...]
W.B.M. is tonight —
10th very cold d[...]
11th was a very rain[...]
morning cleared up a [...]

"Frazer River Thermometer," 1858

Cartoons show the rise and fall of Fraser River Fever in California.

Haida land, Haida gold

Was there gold on the northwest coast? British and American ships travelled to Haida Gwaii (the Queen Charlotte Islands) in 1851 to find out. To the Haida people, this was trespassing. The consequences were explosive. The Haida used hand-made golden bullets to fend off American prospectors. They drove several ships away, and took another ship hostage, burned it and ransomed back the crew.

The British negotiated with the Haida to establish a trading post and mine at Gold Harbour. But Americans were barred. This was a warning to Britain of what was to come during the Fraser River rush.

Race to the starting line

Fraser fever swept first through the continent, then the globe. In one month, the Hudson's Bay Company received "110 pounds [50 kg] of gold dust from the Indians… [prospected] without the aid of anything more than… pans and willow baskets" (*San Francisco Bulletin*, 1858). Papers around the world flashed the news, and the rush was on! Routes were dangerous, and travel was taxing for those swarming in by land or sea.

Overlanders used trade routes from California and other states or pushed west from Canada. Travel by sea was faster — ships competed to be first on the scene. But cholera and scurvy could afflict the gold seekers on board. For some, the mad scramble ended in a lonely grave.

Diary of Samuel Hathaway, 1862

Working to buy provisions, Samuel Hathaway stayed on too late in the season. A boil on his foot crippled him and winter arrived. His last entry: "O, that I were out of this gloomy wretched country! Were I not a cripple I should feel at ease for if snow set in steadily I could pack up & leave, sure of being able to fight my way out, but now my fears get the better of me." Someone then added this line about his death: "By all accounts lost trying to make Williams Creek."

happy for life.— Well, I must grind along
till my lucky day comes, & gather in my
slow dollars one by one, only too happy if
old age don't nip me before I get a
little resting place in this wide world.

Sept. 23.— On Nelson yet. Been scratching
around steadily.— am now even on the cost
of the trip & enough besides to take me
back to Cal². Bad weather now—
snowing & freezing nearly all the time. Most
of the men have left the creek.— only
four left here now, & each one working &
living by himself about a quarter of a mile
from each other. To day my cabin mate
went away. We started in to work together,
but he soon after bought a bit of ground
that was paying well — about $50 a day—

giving $5.00. It fizzled out completely
before he got half his money back, &
now he strikes out for Williams Creek.
Would go myself & try for big diggings, but
I cannot feel justified to leave $10 a day,
& I am making that now with a fair
show of doing so as long as I dare stay
here.— That cannot be many weeks
more.— Looks dubious now.— If a
deep snow comes on it will be a
serious matter for me to get out.
But my chief fear is of being robbed
on my way down,— many have been
robbed & some murdered on the down
trails. This country is all a wilderness
& it is very easy for robbers to escape.
No doubt there are many lying in
wait for the big purses that have been
growing fat up here & will soon be on the
way out for the winter.

RULES

AND

REGULATIONS,

Issued in conformity with the

Gold Field Act, 1859.

5R38

VICTORIA, V. I.,
Printed at the British Colonist Office,
MDCCCLX.

1863?

Rules & Regulations,
issued in conformity with the *Gold Fields Act*, 1859

Hurry up and dash

The world arrived in Victoria, but it didn't stay long. The first ship bringing 800 gold seekers to Fort Victoria in 1858 doubled its population. That summer, 25,000 people landed in Victoria. Everyone came to buy mining permits, then waited for another boat to take them up the Fraser River.

Draft of a free miners licence, 1858

The first gold seekers came from California, then from China, Australia, South America, the United States and Europe. Expecting wilderness, they found at Victoria a vast sea of tents. Inflation was rampant. Land prices rose 4,000% a month. In their race for the gold, some miners built "coffin boats" too frail to survive the journey across the ocean to the mouth of the Fraser.

View of Fort Victoria
(before the gold rush)

Levan Cullison, oil on card, 1890

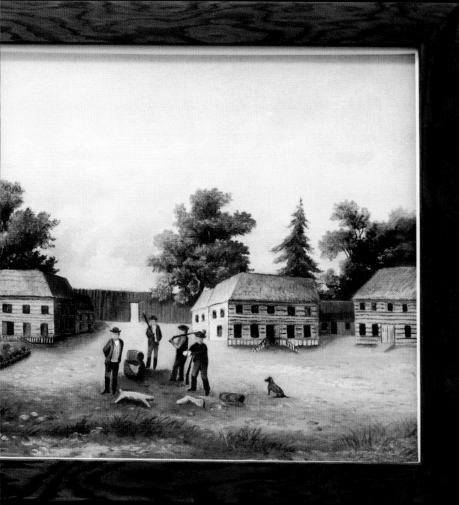

Diary of Richard Carr

Richard Carr (father of artist Emily Carr) made his fortune in California selling provisions to miners.

Victoria transformed

The gold rush transformed Victoria into a miniature San Francisco. Though prospectors moved on, merchants and builders stayed, changing the fur-trading fort forever.

Businessmen with connections to San Francisco raised hundreds of new buildings, opened groceries, hotels and newspapers. Victoria was the largest shipping port in British Columbia until the late 1880s. Speculators drove up land prices and culture blossomed. Norwegians, French, Italians, Chinese, Irish and English thrived in a cosmopolitan economy. Merchant networks were far reaching and powerful — the first building with gas lighting wasn't the Legislature, but a liquor store!

Footbridges to Chinatown

Newly arrived Chinese merchants, remembering California's discrimination, chose to settle at the edge of Fort Victoria. Chinatown was connected to Victoria by three footbridges across a ravine. Tenement houses and businesses grew, recruiting and supplying miners. Canada's first Chinatown was the gateway to the gold fields.

Businesses like Kwong Lee & Co and Tai Soong & Co connected the gold rush trails to trans-Pacific trade. They built stores and warehouses in Victoria and along the trails, running mule and wagon trains all the way to the Cariboo.

Chinatown arch in Victoria, 1870s

Receipts for the transportation of gold dust and cash belonging to the Kwong Lee and Quing Lee Chan companies of Victoria

"You cannot ascend mountains, toward the mining towns or pass from one mining camp to another, without noticing the contrast in the scenes around you to anything you ever saw before... Men met in groups packing their provisions; then a train of Indians... Anon you met throngs of Chinamen packing up the river; they pass and greet you in broken English with, 'how do you do John'... Next comes the Negro, with a polite 'good morning sar,' or Chileano, Mexican or Kanaka [Hawaiian], each with a heavy load."

— *Victoria Gazette*, 1858

"The Piano That Saved Lives"

During the period of the gold rush when armed miners tried to get control of the gold-bearing sand bars on the Fraser River, Grand Chief Dr. Rose Charlie's grandmother owned the only piano in the area. The family believes that because she played this piano, they were left alone.

Waiting for gold and salmon

In April 1858, gold seekers flocked by boat or on horseback to Yale, the last steamboat stop on the Fraser. People crowded into the small town, and prices skyrocketed. Gold seekers bought supplies and waited for the river level to fall enough to uncover gold-bearing gravel bars. First Nations waited for salmon runs to begin. Neither would happen before August.

That summer's arrivals were mostly Americans. They came from California's rush, where violence against First Nations was common. Tensions rose. Waiting meant losing the first opportunities to find gold on the river. Many ran low on money and supplies. Too late, the authorities saw the signs of serious trouble.

The Fraser River war

Clashes between miners and First Nations along the Fraser River began as small conflicts. Miners ignored First Nations fishing rights, seized their gold diggings, stole canoes and insulted local women. Chiefs who protested were insulted, disarmed or captured.

But the narrow rocky canyon north of Yale allowed for stronger resistance. Nlaka'pamux warriors fired guns at miners from the cover of rocks. No one was safe along the narrow banks. Many of those fleeing in canoes drowned in the rapids. Bodies battered by rocks and rapids floated downstream. Seeing the reality of the dispute, the miners wanted to fight their way up the canyon killing any First Nations people in their way.

South of the Fraser, the Yakima Indian War reached a bloody conclusion. American regiments and howitzers shelled Indigenous fighters. First Nations intensely disliked armed American miners who walked north through that war. To the east of the canyon one group looted and massacred an Okanagan village. News spread quickly. First Nations gathered to discuss a war they saw as spreading north, drawn by gold.

Ditch-digging companies on the Fraser River between Fort Hope and Fort Yale, 1858

List of Ditch Companies on Fraser River between Fort Hope & Fort Yale.

1. "Pioneer Ditch Company" — Texas Bar — Recd. Oct 5th 1858
2. "Santa Clara & American Bar Water Co" — American Bar Creek — July 30th 1858
3. " " " " — Creek at head of American Bar " "
4. " " " " — Douglas Creek — " "
5. " " " " — Lake back of Puget Sound Bar " "
6. " " " " — Creek at Fort Hope, N Side — " "
7. "Fort Yale Bar ditch Company" — Fort Yale Creek — " October 1st/58
8. "Ohio Ditch Company" — Rocky point Creek — " 7th 1858
9. "Cornish Bar Ditch Company" — Fort Hope creek — " 7th
10. Wm Curnell & 8 others to a ditch on Hudson's Bar — " "
11. O'Brien, Cook & Wright — to the 1st 2 small creeks below Fort Yale — " 8th
12. " " " — to 2nd water of Fort Yale Creek — " "
13. Hawley & List — creek 3/4 of a mile above Strawbury Isld — " 9th
14. "Trinity Bar Ditch Co" — Trinity Bar creek — " 11th
15. "Posey Bar Ditch Co" — creek 1/2 mile above Strawbury Isld sp — " 12th
16. "Perrier Ditch Co" — creek 1 1/2 miles below Hills Bar — " "
17. "London creek Ditch Co" — opposite Emerys Bar — " 14th
18. "French Bar water Co" — creek at French Bar — " 18th
19. "Cataract water Co" — 1/2 miles below Hills Bar — " 22nd
20. "Trafalgar creek water Co" — Trafalgar creek, 4 miles ab: F:Hope — " 23rd
21. "Hills Bar Ditch Co" — creek back of Hills Bar — " 25th

Of the above — 13 are finished and in operation
7 " nearly finished.
1. just been granted.

Indian

No 1

Frazer River, Fort Yale, August 28th 1858

To His Excellency
James Douglass
Governor of Vancouvers Island
Dear Sir

Having Just returned from a short
campaign up to Thompson River, to suppress
the out breaks of the indians, That That occured
on Frazer River. It had become so alarming
that the miners had been Driven from their
claims from with in fourteen miles of the forks
as far down as to the Indian Rancheries
twelve miles above this place. In fact I was in-
forming was the news from above That hundreds
were leaving this place to returne to their homes
My Resolution was soon made. and I will now
procede to give you an abstract of my plan and
proceeding. On the 16th of the same month
a company was formed to procede at once
up the river. And by a unanimous vote I
was elected their Captain. being delayed in
making our arrangements. we did not
leave this place until the Morning of the 19th
two miles from this place. We came to a halt

Captain Snyder's letter to Governor James Douglas

This letter, dated August 28, 1858, explains how Captain Snyder made peace with the Nlaka'pamux.

The colony of British Columbia, created in part to deal with the war, struggled to prevent further bloodshed. Some miners and First Nations leaders drafted peace treaties. But many relationships built during the fur trade collapsed. The great number of miners arriving on the Fraser overwhelmed the native inhabitants.

Journey to peace

American Henry Snyder didn't want war. But many gold-seekers continued to form militia groups that, he said, "wished to proceed and kill every man, woman and child that… had Indian blood in them."

Under Chief Spintlum, the Nlaka'pamux blockaded the Fraser River and drove foreign miners out. Hundreds of warriors assembled at Lytton. Other First Nations, including the Okanagan and Secwepemc, promised support. While many chiefs favoured continued war, Spintlum urged a ceasefire. Finally, Snyder, elected Commander of the Companies at a mass miners' meeting, journeyed north. Together, he and Spintlum negotiated a peace treaty.

Gold rush guns

Gold miners in California, Australia and British Columbia all carried similar weapons: small handguns of all types. They used them for self-defence and to protect their claim and their gold.

Gold-rush pistols predate those seen in Hollywood westerns. The Colt percussion cap pistol fired a lead ball when the cap ignited powder behind it. Reloading was slow. The first modern cartridge, the .22 Short, became available in 1857 and is still sold today.

Percussion rifles gave way to repeating rifles with brass cartridges: first the .44 calibre Henry and then the popular Winchester Model 1866. The Sioux used Henrys at Little Bighorn. If British Columbia's gold rush had been a decade later, the new firearms would have made the Fraser River war worse than it was.

Revolvers

From top to bottom: Samuel Colt Model 1851 Navy Colt (London made) percussion revolver, 1853–56; Colt 7 shot, .22 calibre revolver, 1871; Ely Whitney civilian Navy Model .36 calibre percussion revolver, 1860; Pin fire revolver, .32 calibre, 1850–70.

Hard roads to gold

How would you travel along a wild river canyon? Imagine a road just 2 metres wide at the edge of a cliff above a raging river. Gold-seekers travelled north along the Cariboo Wagon Road with wagons, mules, horses and even wheelbarrows. One false step could be fatal.

Some used other routes, over mountains from all directions. But thousands used the treacherous Cariboo Wagon Road. Crossing one third of British Columbia, it connected Yale to Barkerville in 1865. The road was surveyed by the British Royal Engineers, who came to build settlements and infrastructure in 1858. They mapped gold regions, planned town sites and blasted through some of the roughest land on Earth.

China Bar Bluff on the Cariboo Wagon Road, 1867 or 1868

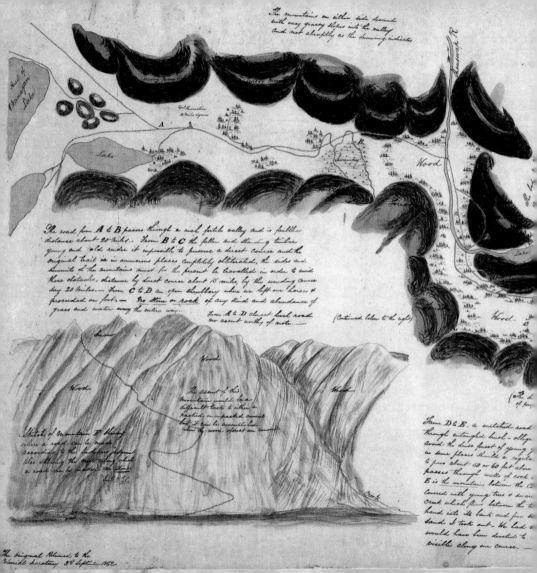

The mountains on either side descend with easy grassy slopes into the valley and not abruptly as the drawing indicates

Head of Okanagan Lake

Lake

A

B

Wood

Forest

Lake

Thompson R.

The road from A to B passes through a rich fertile valley and is perfectly level distance about 20 miles. — From B to C the fallen and standing timber young and old render it impossible to preserve a direct course and the original trail is in numerous places completely obliterated, the sides and summits of the mountains must for the present be travelled in order to avoid these obstacles, distance by direct course about 15 miles, by the winding course say 20 miles. — From C to D an open shrubbery where we left our horses & proceeded on foot. — No stone or rock of any kind and abundance of grass and water nearly the entire way.

From A to D almost level road no ascent worthy of note. —

(Continued below to the right)

Snow

Wood

Wood

Wood

The ascent of this mountain would be a difficult task to within a practicle or unpacked animal but it can be accomplished when the wood &c are removed

Sketch of mountain E shewing where a road can be made according to the surface proposed. Also shewing the only way in which a road can be made — no stone

Creek

From D to E, a... road through entangled bush — oblige around the dense forest of young... in some places thinks a regular to pass about 50 or 60 feet above... passes through walls of rock. E is the mountain between the C... Covered with young trees & so are creek which flow between the two hand into its bank and force to hand I took out — We had... would have been devoted to visible along our course. —

The Original Returned to the Colonial Secretary 3rd September 1852.

of Proposed road between
of Okanagan Lake and
Columbia River. —

W.G. Cox
8th August 1862

"Map of proposed road between Head of Okanagan Lake and the Columbia River" [tracing]

W. G. Cox, August 8, 1862
As reproduced by Lt. Corporal James Conroy R.E.,
December 3, 1862

Indian Map

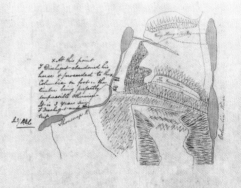

The plateau of mountain E is
represented by my Guides as being an open
plain of about one day's half journey for
packed animals the descent is gradual and
not practicable.

Between the termination of the mountain
and the Columbia River a dense forest of
young trees but no timber. One day for packed
Animals supposing the trail to be free from
impediment.

This is from Indian information

Wood

Middle Lake Columbia River

x At this point
I Dischief abandoned his
horse & proceeded to the
Columbia on foot — the
timber being perfectly
impassable Mountains
for a young man
I think of some
trifle

"Miners, composed of many nations, British subjects, Americans, French, Germans, Danes, Africans and Chinese... volunteered their services immediately on our wish to open a practicable route into the interior... An Engineer with guides and Indians acquainted with the country, blazes the trees; and marks out the road."

— **Governor Douglas to Lord Stanley,**
   The Colonial Despatches of Vancouver Island and British Columbia 1846–1871, **August 1858**

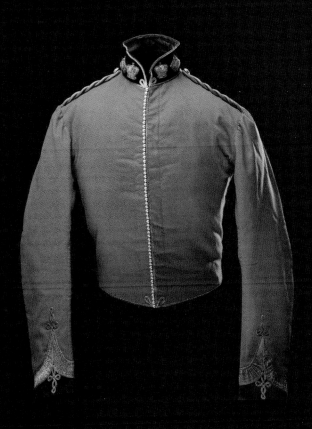

Dress jacket and vest of Colonel Richard Moody, commander of the Royal Engineers

The Royal Engineers

Royal Engineers were selected for the sensitive diplomatic task of building and supporting a colony in close proximity to the United States. A symbol of the British Empire, they influenced law and order, but fought no battles and routed no enemies. Instead, they surveyed, mapped and built towns, such as New Westminster, and built roads over almost impossible terrain.

When the British government withdrew the Royal Engineers, many of its ranks resigned to stay in British Columbia. Some took land-grant pensions. They ran hotels, farms and businesses. Engineer Richard Wolfenden, for example, became the Queen's Printer for the new colony and later the province.

Astronomical transit used by Captain Parsons of the Royal Engineers, 1860s

The Cariboo Wagon Road

How long is the Cariboo Wagon Road? It is hard to say. The oldest section was the Harrison Lake route, from the Fraser River to Port Douglas (on the northern tip of the lake) and northeast to Lillooet. The old Cariboo toll road began at Lillooet. Each road house, such as 70 Mile House or 100 Mile House, is measured from Lillooet.

Gustavus Blin Wright built more than half of the Cariboo Wagon Road. In 1861, he built a toll road from Lillooet north to Clinton (47 Mile House). The next year, Governor Douglas hired him to extend the road north to Fort Alexandria (now Alexandria, on the Fraser River south of Quesnel).

At Soda Creek, he built a steamer to take miners to Quesnel where trails led overland to the gold fields of Quesnelle Forks, Horsefly, Richfield and Barkerville. In the Fraser Canyon, the Royal Engineers blasted rock and created a new Cariboo route from Yale, along the Fraser, and over Pavilion Mountain to Clinton.

Stagecoach

William Ballou began the first express company to the gold fields. Francis Barnard started a pony express service in 1861, adding wagons and buying Jaffray's Fraser River Express. Barnard connected with the Dietz and Nelson stagecoach, which ran between Lillooet and Yale. Winning the government mail contract, Barnard added winter sleds and larger stagecoaches. By 1867 Barnard Express controlled the service from Victoria to Barkerville.

The first stagecoaches and horses came from California. Later, stagecoaches were made at Ashcroft. Horses were specially trained in Vernon for pulling coaches. Roadhouses every 18 miles supplied meals and fresh horses along the four-day trip.

British Columbia Express Company stagecoach

Recovered from the bush, this stagecoach has been restored by the Historic O'Keefe Ranch, founded during the British Columbia gold rush.

Welcome to the Cariboo

Was the mother lode in the Cariboo? The rush extended hundreds of kilometres north along the Fraser River. In the 1860s, prospectors used Cornish methods to mine deeply buried Cariboo gold. They built water wheels and sluicing systems, cutting down forests and diverting rivers and creeks, scarring the landscape.

The richest creeks became legendary — Williams, Antler, Grouse. Huge fortunes were made and lost by men like Billy Barker and "Cariboo" Cameron. Instant towns appeared — Barkerville, Likely, Richfield. Immigrants from many backgrounds formed new companies, pooling resources. But the merchants became the richest of them all.

A commonwealth desired

Before the rush, fur traders built strong relationships with First Nations. No one wanted a repeat of California and Australia's gold-rush violence. After the Fraser River war, the British government instructed the new colony's governor, James Douglas, to protect First Nations from the rush's worst effects.

Faced with discrimination in California, Black Americans came north. To many, the lands north of the 49th parallel appeared to offer economic opportunities and freedom.

Douglas intended British Columbia to be an inclusive commonwealth, with "equality before the law." The colony was vast, the new laws imperfectly realized. His vision, though far-sighted, turned out to be short-lived.

"Nor will Her Majesty's Government undervalue the claims and services of the Indians, Negroes, Half-castes of all complexions or Asiatics, who, maltreated or excluded in the United States will again repair to a land, we trust of irreproachable equality and freedom."

— Lord Napier, British Minister to the United States, to Lord Malmesbury, Foreign Secretary, July 30, 1858, HBC Archives

"They [First Nations] should be treated in all respects as Her Majesty's other subjects; and that the local Magistrates would tend to their complaints, and guard them from wrong... I strove to make them conscious that they were recognized members of the Commonwealth."

— Governor Douglas to Newcastle, *The Colonial Despatches of Vancouver Island and British Columbia 1846–1871*, October 9, 1860

"In California... we were powerless to appeal to law for protection. British Columbia... gave protection and equality of political privileges. I cannot describe with what joy we hailed the opportunity to enjoy that liberty."

— Mifflin Gibbs, Black community leader, 1858

Big dreams, high prices

A gold seeker's life was tough. Living in a tent, working from dawn to dusk, hoping provisions would last the short season, you dreamed of El Dorado's riches. Life revolved around the river's gravel bars or the diggings.

An occasional trek to town was a chance to have a bath, eat better grub, visit the saloon and maybe dance a little. Prices were extreme: $12 for a dozen eggs when wages were a dollar a day. As gold rush communities matured, towns looked more like home. Barkerville eventually built a library, a hospital, a theatre, two churches and many saloons.

Gold digger, BC

William G. R. Hind, oil on board, 1864

Women in the gold fields

Gold-rush society wasn't for the faint of heart. Few women travelled to the gold fields, and those who did had to have an escort. Some women disguised themselves for safety. Harriet Collins became "Harry," a young man looking for his brother. Harry was actually searching for her husband. She was also pregnant. Her cover was blown when she gave birth.

Parasol

This parasol was used by gold rush entrepreneur Jane Wilcox from 1858 to 1862.

Silk taffeta dress, c. 1860

This dress belonged to a woman in the Pemberton family.

Women worked in laundries and restaurants, as saloon or hotel keepers, investors or prostitutes. But their life stories — like those of most gold-seekers — remain elusive, both for those who fared well and those who didn't.

Gold rush merchant networks

Need some French champagne, English toffee or Chinese tea? Gold-rush merchants were your connection to the wider world. Merchants — whether Black, Jewish, Chinese or British — created networks abroad and community at home.

They fundraised for churches, fire departments, libraries and hospitals. Organizations like the Freemasons and Odd Fellows provided the permanent core to a transient society.

Scholars today are studying the networks merchants created. Whether you needed specialty goods or to bring a body back home, merchants linked the world.

Gold Rush Commission Agent sign

Henry Nathan Jr. operated a general store and commission agency in Victoria. At his store, miners could stock up on supplies and obtain a mining license. Victoria later elected Mr. Nathan the first Jewish Member of the House of Commons in 1871.

Chinese Freemasons

Chinese miners in Barkerville persevered despite racial discrimination. They often worked for lower wages or on abandoned claims, calling this 翻沙屎 ("flipping through sand dung"). Many joined the Chinese Freemasons, Canada's oldest Chinese organization. Founded in Barkerville's goldfields in 1863, the Freemasons helped new arrivals, provided hostels and meeting places, and protected members. The Freemasons adopted a Western symbol for their organization. But they followed the structure and rules of the secret Hong Men societies of China.

Chinese labourer outfit made of mud silk

"Cantonese Pacific" and "Pacific Canada"

The British used "Canton" to refer to both Guangdong, the province from which most early Chinese migrants came, and Guangzhou, the capital of Guangdong. The recurrent pattern of early Chinese migration for the gold mountains across the Pacific has been termed by Dr. Henry Yu (University of British Columbia) as the "Cantonese Pacific."

As a result of the gold rushes, migrants speaking various dialects of Cantonese influenced cultures of the trans-Pacific world. The engagement of migrants from Asia, Europe and other parts of the Americas with each other and with First Peoples historically provides a "Pacific Canada" perspective.

Bust by 1865

Placer gold became scarce on the Fraser and in the Cariboo by the mid-1860s. To delay the inevitable, the colonial government built roads through the interior, plunging itself into debt. Prospectors searched creek after creek, exploring almost every part of British Columbia. But El Dorado was an ever-receding dream.

The gold-seekers moved on — some to other rushes, some back home. But many miners stayed to log, fish, farm or ranch, helping the colony move toward Confederation. British Columbia joined Canada in 1871. The gold rush created the province and its resource-based economy. But the rush's lasting legacy brought even greater change.

American annexation

Many Americans wanted more than just British Columbia's gold. For good reasons, the colonial government worried about American annexation.

American agents worked to protect US interests on the Fraser River. American miners bristled at British attitudes, taxes and mining regulations. Ned McGowan's miners plotted to seize Hudson's Bay Company forts on the Fraser. McGowan hoped to build support for US expansion that would include all of the Fraser River.

But in the end, American and British military surveyors cooperated. Together, they blazed the border from the Prairies to the Pacific.

Lancet and wallet

Reverend John Sheepshanks walked to the gold fields with this smallpox inoculation kit. He inoculated the people of the Xaxli'p First Nation and learned a year later that, unlike many, they had survived.

People and lands forever altered

For First Nations, the land holds stories. The gold rush changed the land: erasing names, landmarks and sacred places. It also changed people: forcing First Nations who lived along the rivers onto reserves, changing their traditional diets and decimating their populations with smallpox and flu.

Two-day chronometer, 1858

This two-day chronometer was used by the Royal Engineers to establish British Columbia's border with the United States.

Road-building continued after the rush, creating new routes but destroying old trails. The railway arrived. Chinese, Scottish, Mexican and other ethnicities settled throughout British Columbia. Towns sprouted and grew. Victoria became the province's capital. But environmental destruction continued, brought on by industrial mining, logging and drilling for oil and gas. El Dorado's golden thread had laid a grid over the land.

A claim on the land

Searching for a new El Dorado, the world made huge claims on British Columbia. Miners claimed First Nations' lands; settlers claimed territory for agriculture; industries claimed resources. The costs were high.

But unlike other gold rushes, the British Columbia rush offered a brighter legacy. The fur trade provided a setting for stronger partnerships, respect and diversity. The Fraser Canyon peace treaty averted a war.

Still, the repercussions of the gold rush resonate to this day. Conflicts over First Nations land rights continue, and the pursuit of El Dorado endures with oil, natural gas and mineral exploration.

The Chilcotin War

In 1864, the year that James Douglas retired as governor of the colony, businessman Alfred Waddington began constructing a new road from the coast to the Cariboo. As his road crews progressed across the Chilcotin Plateau, they encountered resistance from Tsilhqot'in First Nations who lived there. The crews threatened the Tsilhqot'in people and mistreated their women.

In April, Tsilhqot'in Chief Klatsassin and his warriors attacked road workers and settlers, killing 19 of them. The new governor, Frederick Seymour, sent an armed response and forced a standoff. In August, the colonial government invited six Tsilhqot'in chiefs to Fort Chilcotin, promising peace talks. But when the chiefs arrived they were arrested, tried and convicted of murder. Five chiefs were hanged in October; the sixth, the following July.

To The High Sheriff of
British Columbia

Whereas   Telloot
            Klatsassin
            Piell
            Tahpit
     and   Chessus

were on or about the twenty eighth
day of September now last
past duly convicted before
Matthew Baillie Begbie
Esquire Judge of The Supreme
Court of Civil Justice of British
Columbia one of Her Majestys
Justices of the Peace for
the said Colony at Quesnelle
Mouth in the said Colony
and duly sentenced to death

Now

Death warrant for Tsilhqot'in Chiefs Telloot, Klatsassin, Piell, Tahpit and Chessus, 1864

Legacy of the Chiefs

The Tsilhqot'in never forgot the colony's betrayal. For 150 years they fought for justice. In June 2014, the Supreme Court of Canada confirmed the Tsilhqot'in title to 1,900 square kilometres in central British Columbia. In October 2014, British Columbia's premier formally apologized for the execution of the six Tsilhqot'in chiefs. For Chief Roger Williams, it was an emotional end to "unfinished business."

Barkerville

Since its founding, Barkerville has been the heart and soul of the Cariboo gold fields. It was named after Billy Barker, who discovered gold on Williams Creek in 1861 and then struck it rich the following year. Barker and his partners dug deep into the clay beds near Stouts Gulch and, on August 17, 1862, broke through to an ancient creek below. The men filled their buckets with 60 ounces (1.7 kilograms) of gold nuggets. Instantly wealthy and spending freely, Barker became famous.

The town of Barkerville sprung up along Williams Creek and the buried ancient creek bed. It soon housed 5,000 residents, including a large Chinese community, and became the economic, social and government hub of the Cariboo. Some called Barkerville the biggest city north of San Francisco and west of Chicago.

By 1944, Barkerville's population had dropped to 122. Major restoration began in 1958. Today, with its resident businesses and historical interpreters, Barkerville is one of the world's pre-eminent historic towns.

William (Billy) Barker (1817–1894)

Billy Barker spent all the money he earned from his big strike and never found any more gold. He died penniless in Victoria in 1894.

Barkerville, 1868

This photo depicts the main street of Barkerville just before the 1868 fire that destroyed the town.

Barkerville today

The town's actors are portraying miners in front of a Cornish wheel.

One ounce, .9999 gold maple leaf bullion coin

EVERYTHING OLD IS NEW AGAIN

Is anyone not touched by gold? Gold is vital to science and technology. Orbiting satellites contain gold. The two *Voyager* spacecraft launched in 1977 carry with them a golden message to the stars.

Since gold was discovered 6,000 years ago, it hasn't lost its allure. From wedding rings to Olympic medals, gold is a standard we use to express honour and respect, excellence and love.

The search for more gold is global. Mining companies rework old claims and explore new finds. The world constantly feels mining's environmental impacts.

You're as good as gold

Think of gold medals, golden moments or a golden age. If you're golden, you're demonstrating excellence or outstanding success. We use the metaphor of gold to convey high standards in almost every facet of life.

Gold Rush Trail, near historic Fort Yale

For over 150 years, thousands of tourists have followed the Gold Rush Trail north from Hope and Yale through the Fraser Canyon to Barkerville. These people do not seek gold — instead, they take in the dramatic scenery and explore the communities founded during the gold rush. The trail remains one of the world's most alluring pathways of exploration and an amazing aspect of Canadian heritage.

Maurice Richard's Montreal Canadiens Stanley Cup championship ring, 1959

Gold record presented to Keith Scott

Keith Scott was the guitarist on the 1984 Bryan Adams album *Reckless*. Recorded in Vancouver *Reckless* was the first Canadian album to exceed domestic sales of 1 million copies. It has sold an astounding 12 million copies worldwide.

A friend of art and science

Work is easy when gold's involved. Roll it into sheets or draw it into fine wire. Carve it, pound it or melt it and cast it into forms. Gold needs little polishing and its softness resists breakage. If you're an artist, you work gold in pure form or bond it with other metals for strength or colour.

Gold cathode radio tube

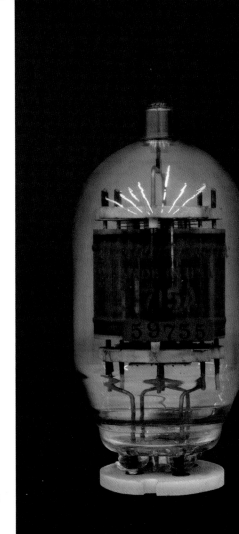

If you're a scientist, gold is also your friend. It easily conducts electricity and doesn't tarnish, and its chemistry is stable. There are tiny amounts of gold in your cell phone, computer and television.

Rocket payload particle collector

Gold's uses in technology

Gold's purity makes it the preferred metal for innovative engineers. Gold conducts electricity and resists corrosion in the harshest environments.

Thirty grams (about an ounce) of gold can make a thin sheet of 9 square metres to deflect radiation in outer space or to protect office windows on Earth. It can also make a wire, 20 times thinner than human hair, that stretches for 80 kilometres.

Medical scientists use gold in diagnostic equipment and implants for the inner ear or eyelid. Doctors have found it useful in treating malaria and cancerous tumours. And nanotechnology scientists are also exploring new uses for gold.

Gold plate alleged to be of 99.998 fineness

Stamped with a crown and "Royal Mint – Ottawa," 1912.

Gold as a commodity

When trading gold, precise measurement creates an exchange you can trust. We measure precious metals (gold, silver, platinum) using an ancient Roman system. A troy ounce (31.1034768 g) is 10% heavier than a regular (avoirdupois) ounce.

Small amounts of gold are measured in grains, as is gunpowder. To detect fraud, experts use electricity, chemicals and combinations of volume, diameter and weight.

Highly refined bars stamped for purity have replaced crude-cast gold-rush bars. Small investment gold bars are precisely cut from refined sheets. But today, most investors find electronic and paper methods easier than trading in actual gold.

Royal Canadian Mint
MNT, MNT.U *First day of trading:* Tuesday November 29, 2011

Official engraving marking the issuance of $600 million worth
of gold exchange-traded receipts on the Toronto Stock Exchange

$5 and $10 gold circulation coin set, 1912–1914

Coin of the realm

The Gold Standard linked a country's money to a set amount of gold. By 1890, fixed exchange rates applied when trading paper bills for gold coins. In 1908, Britain created the Canadian branch of its Royal Mint to supply a growing Canada with domestic coinage as well as to refine gold from the Klondike rush and later from mines in Timmins, Ontario.

Is there enough gold to cover every business transaction in the world? There isn't! Today, most nations don't link currency to gold reserves. What would replace it? One country's currency? Bitcoin? Not everyone agrees. Today, gold is a free-floating commodity still filled with mystique.

El Dorado's myth still pulls

Three quarters of the world's gold-mining and exploration companies are Canadian. But today we find most gold beneath the ground in other countries. China, Australia, the United States, Russia and South Africa lead the pack. Indonesia's Grasberg mine (which also produces copper) is among the world's largest, employing 20,000 people!

The "Million Dollar" 100 kilogram .99999 pure gold Maple Leaf coin

In 2007, the Royal Canadian Mint officially launched the world's first 99.999% pure-gold bullion coin. It contains 100 kilograms or 3,215 troy ounces of pure gold and has a face value of $1,000,000. The coin was designed by Royal Canadian Mint artist and Senior Engraver Stan Witten; the other side bears the effigy of Queen Elizabeth II by celebrated Canadian portrait artist Susanna Blunt. In October 2007, Guinness World Records certified this coin as the world's largest gold coin. Five of these coins have since been purchased by investors from Canada and abroad.

Modern mining ventures dwarf everything that has come before. But these giant operations aren't without controversy. Disputes over mining regulations and Indigenous rights continue. Environmental costs trigger passionate public debates.

The compulsion continues

Our obsession with finding gold in the New World started with a story of El Dorado, told and retold until it became a global myth. And the myth hasn't faltered in over 500 years.

El Dorado spurred gold rushes that drove great migrations and reshaped populations around the world. The Fraser River rush created the multicultural province we now know as British Columbia.

Today, gold rushes continue to transform areas of the world with the construction of roads and instant camps, with environmental damage and with impacts on Indigenous peoples and politics, just like it did during British Columbia's rush.

El Dorado, is it myth or reality? No matter which, our fascination endures. And gold itself will endure even longer.

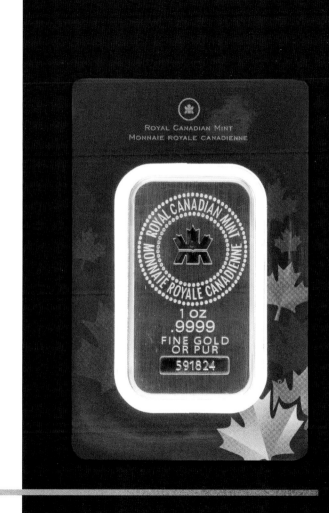

One ounce gold wafer

"Kilobottle" of gold grain: 32,148 ounces, 99.999% pure gold

ACKNOWLEDGEMENTS

The following organizations and individuals have graciously agreed to loan important artifacts for this exhibition, some of which have been included in this publication:

- Art Gallery of Greater Victoria
- Bank of Canada Museum, Currency Collection
- Barkerville Historic Town
- Reg Beck (private lender)
- Canada Science and Technology Museum
- Crocker Art Museum
- David Foster Foundation
- Jim Erickson (private lender)
- Government House (British Columbia)
- Historic O'Keefe Ranch
- Grant Keddie (private lender)
- Kate Kerr (private lender)
- Land Title and Survey Authority of BC
- Metropolitan Museum of Art
- National Gallery of Australia
- Oakland Museum of California
- Quesnel & District Museum & Archives
- Royal Canadian Mint
- San Francisco Maritime National Historical Park
- Keith Scott (private lender)
- South Cariboo Historical Museum Society
- Art Vickers (private lender)
- Yale and District Historical Society

Photo Credits

Courtesy of the Royal BC Museum and Archives

p. 4	A-00353 / Photo: Frederick Dally	**p. 67**	E/B/H28 2
p. 8	A-00558 / Photo: Frederick Dally	**p. 68**	NWs 971.35 B862g
p. 13	990.65.15	**p. 69**	GR-1104
p. 18	13902a,b	**p. 70**	PDP02175
p. 20	990.65.13, 990.65.14, 990.65.16	**p. 72**	MS-0610
p. 32	PDP02292	**p. 75**	E-01926
p. 34	NWs 971M C821	**p. 76**	GR-1372
p. 37	964.3495.6a	**p. 81**	GR-1770
p. 40	K/EA/C43	**p. 82**	GR-1372, Box 126:1617
p. 43	2014.188.1, 2014.188.2	**p. 85**	965.2491.1a-c, 2012.292.2, 966.26.1, 972.273.1
p. 45	972.4.5	**p. 86**	A-03867 / Photo: Frederick Dally
p. 46	PDP02612	**p. 91**	HH2015.60.1
p. 49	971.244.1A-H, 972.4.73	**p. 92**	965.3003.1
p. 51	PDP00032	**p. 102**	PDP00026
p. 52	990.65.1	**p. 104**	2003.14.1
p. 56	A-3570 / Photo: Charles Gentile	**p. 105**	975.110.7A-B
p. 59	965.2067.1	**p. 107**	HH1988.6.1
p. 62	MS-0843	**p. 108**	964.3658.1, 964.3661.1
p. 64	NWs 971.35F F848 O/S		